5⁰⁰

THE GARDEN
BENCH

THE LIBRARY *of* GARDEN DETAIL

THE GARDEN
BENCH

MIRABEL OSLER

PAVILION

First published in 1991 by
Pavilion Books Limited
196 Shaftesbury Avenue, London WC2H 8JL

Photographic credits listed on page 63

Designed by Paul Burcher

A CIP catalogue records for this book is available from
The British Library

ISBN 1 85145 785 2

Printed and bound in Italy by L.E.G.O., Vicenza

10   9   8   7   6   5   4   3   2   1

CONTENTS

6

*I*NTRODUCTION

SITTING IN YOUR OWN GARDEN IS A FEAT TO BE WORKED at with unflagging determination and single-mindedness – for what gardener worth his salt sits down? I am proposing here that you stop in your tracks and reconsider your garden from a totally new angle; perhaps not prone – but certainly from a relaxed position, for the seating arrangements in a garden require commitment and fine-honed discrimination.

Have you ever noticed how few sitting places you find in private gardens? How seldom the versatility and importance of benches is considered? True gardeners, with their peerless taste, dexterity and inspired planting, never stop. Perhaps the only concession to momentary sloth can be seen outside the french windows where the one seat is placed looking out towards the garden – with the phone and drinks handy. Guilt is a great tyrant. To sit is almost an offence, a sign of depravity and an outrage towards every felicitous refinement which has gone to making the garden. So this book is intended to persuade – to encourage a contrary attitude and to sharpen physical and visual awareness of a whole world of subtleties.

Before the sixteenth century, figures in the garden sat poetically on scented banks, turfed benches or in flowery meads – seldom an unalloyed pleasure considering our wayward summer climate. Nowadays the variety of benches and the way in which we use them allow for infinite possibilities. Material, shape, comfort and height can each, when used sensitively, enchance an appreciation of the garden in a way previously unimagined. There are seats for languor, for conversation or for tactical alighting; there are others for artistic 'placement' or as jokes and outlandish contrivances; there are contemplative seats for the pensive, convivial sitting where shoulder nudges shoulder; seats for scents, secrecy, twilight or shelter. Equally important are 'strategic' benches – benches positioned where their design, prominence or lure have a forceful voice. Imagine winter: for though in Cumbria or in Maine no one will be out lolling on a bench in December, think of glancing out from the

1. *A stone seat which fits comfortably under a Norway weeping-spruce hybrid* (Picea abies pendula).

warmth indoors and seeing a seat turned to a cipher by deep unblemished snow. Or on a day when gloom lies like a migraine across the landscape, what serenity to see the solid outlines of a stone seat, its dismal patina integrated with the neutrality of the garden. Seats are not merely functional pauses for the weary or a place in the shade when chums come to luncheon.

I am deeply committed to sitting in the garden. Wherever we have lived it has been thoughts of sitting which have stirred my restlessness long before I began fretting over flowers. In our 1½ acres of garden in Shropshire we have thirteen quite specific places; in the Far East where we lived in a wooden house on legs beside the river, we had a seat dropping twenty feet from a rain tree. There I could swing out over the water and look up to where wild orchids, glowing like bullion, festooned the branches overhead. When the drains of the town became too effusive we placed a seat beside a frangipani tree. Here the claustrophobic scent of those white flowers over-whelmed our senses while we had a distant view of canna lilies as pellucid as boiled sweets.

The siting of a bench is critical. However exquisite and carefully chosen the object may be – whether made from

stone, iron or wood – if it is ineptly placed its whole
purpose can be destroyed. Not only should the bench blend
with its surroundings, but height too is crucial. A low seat
placed amongst your flowers may give you a bee's outlook
on borage (*Borago*), or a glimpse through a mist of

2. *Here the curved seat appears to grow*
out of the wall.

11

thalictrums to variations of blue from distant delphiniums.
Or if you have a slope or can contrive a mound or place
your bench on a slightly raised base, you instantly see your
garden from a fascinating vantage. We may not all have a
terrace from which to look down on a geometric design as

at Hatfield House in Hertfordshire, but a glance at the floral choreography seen from a raised position at the Château du Pontrancart near Dieppe is a potent incentive to experiment with height. In our garden I wanted a bird's-eye view, so we built a wooden platform with two seats reached by a double flight of steps. From here in spring we look down on lily-flowering tulips in the meadow and in summer have an aerial vision of effervescent old roses. The cleft oak from which the seats and platform are made adds natural grace to its position, slung high up between two alders, and in winter its silvery structure becomes confused with a tangle of twigs.

12

Some benches are visually important even though they can never be sat upon because they have long since rotted into frailty, leaving a skeleton form as brittle as the cast-off skin of a dragonfly. On the outskirts of a town I once saw the sagging outlines of an ordinary municipal iron seat long past use, where its rusting framework was overgrown with buttercups and meadow-sweet. How beautiful. Imagine coming across that in some unfrequented corner of a garden. Rosemary Verey in her impeccable garden at Barnsley had a bench where no one sat because she had let great purple heads of sweet rocket thrust through the slats.

3. *Not all benches have to be sat on. The visual importance of garden seats is shown by this one, decaying and encrusted with lichen.*

There are innumerable reasons that may dictate the placing of a bench. Why not begin with scent? Choose for high summer, when the place is turbulent with colour, some calm eye of the garden where there are whites and

14

4. *An imposing seat in contrast to the ebullience
of spring.*

creams and ivories, soft blues and dim pinks – all those pale plants which particularly at twilight lavish their sweetness on moths, beetles and humans. Your bench for summer evening scents should be enclosed by trailing branches where roses and honeysuckles are within grasp, where *Lilium regale* and trumpet-shaped tobacco flowers *(Nicotiana sylvestris)* are profligate with scent. Or at midday choose a small perching bench for a brief pause to savour the redolence of thyme, cistus and rosemary. A rustic type of segmented wooden seat could encircle the trunk of a balsam poplar *(Populus balsamifera)* whose aromatic leaves as they unfold fill the air with the essence of spring; or sit under a pendent silver lime *(Tilia petiolaris)* whose dull white flowers with their drowsy fragrance overcome the bees till they succumb to indolence among the grass.

Another choice, extravagant and generous, is for a precise time of the year or hour of the day. Sunset is obvious. But for instance there is blossom. If you have a gnarled and ancient fruit tree, long past its prime, there will

15

still be a season when the dark branches are laden with flowers, and an unadorned seat from which to admire the blossom, underlines the perfection of the moment – for the rest of the year you forget it. Or if you have water in the

5. *A bench floating over a surface of bluebells. This is a good use of an unemphatic place to pause while walking through the wood.*

garden there may be a particular hour when reflections of trees or plants lie clearly across the surface so that sitting there becomes a deliberate appraisal. There are hours for shadows, there is a time for stupor, there are weeks for falling leaves. Then there are all the places to sit when one

16

particular plant is supreme: under a *Magnolia* x *highdownensis* in full flight, you can gaze into the maroon eyes of their dangling flowers; in front of a group of abrasive red hot pokers *(Kniphofia)* which, when carefully sited, can be histrionic; to quietly contemplate a transitory single-petalled rose, *Rosa pimpinellifolia*, or marvel at a galaxy of snowdrops. For even in winter when frost outlines brittle seed-heads there may come an unexpected day of wan sunlight when to sit is a bracing experience.

17

6. *This simple wooden rocker makes an enticing autumn seat.*

Choosing and siting a bench in a small town garden requires meticulous consideration. You cannot clutter a small back yard with furniture, but you could be aberrant and put one seat where you look back at your garden.

Easily movable chairs are also essential, whatever the size of the garden, though I am not yet reconciled to those hybrid affairs – half seat, half wheelbarrow. Their mongrel appearance does not look right unless they are delicately made like the jade green one with two small iron wheels and unobtrusive handles which sits on a terrace of Powis Castle in Wales. But the variety of portable chairs is infinite, from contorted oak, twisted chestnut or tangled saplings; others, comfy and lightweight, are made of basketweave, rattan and canvas; tactile seats of reeded wrought iron; small metal folding chairs or sturdier wooden ones, practical for sitting round a table. To leave the threshold of a house and see a distant group of unoccupied chairs, is as reassuring as the purr of a cat.

18

Though I do not go all the way with that wonderfully acerbic Irish gardener and writer, William Robinson, who stated, 'It is rare to see a garden seat that is not an eyesore', I do think seats can be a blemish. And not just those made of plastic, but the white ones – those stark intrusions which eclipse the harmony of flowers; which pull at the corner of your sight by their garish blatancy, or when grouped

19

7. *Here the handsome white bench eclipses the stone urn in the centre and the pale sprinkling of* Viola cornuta *and pinks – a quieter colour would have been perfect.*

8. Imagine this painted white! Lose the jungle colour, and the originality and charm would disappear.

together in a set of white dining furniture, dominate the prospect so that only by holding up your hand to hide them, can you appreciate the fairness of the garden.

Alas, there are far too many places in the world where a garden is spoiled just because the seat has been painted white. One glimpse at alternatives would stimulate options: the blue-black benches under roses in the Jardins Kahn in Paris;

the slate-blue iron seats against copper beeches at Hidcote; a cinnabar bench in the William Paca Garden in Annapolis are just three examples of the painted seat idyllic in its setting, and each has an additional bonus in that the colours will mellow with advancing years.

Naturally there are places where a white bench does look perfect: surrounded by formal topiary or parterres or in a predominantly green garden; in those parts of North America where white picket fences are an integral part of the scene or in colonial gardens of the south; on terraces and roof gardens; in humble back yards where white trellis hides the surroundings; in cities where the garden is often treated as an extended room to the house; and, most prettily, when seen against a wash of white cosmos as lightweight as a water-colour.

9. *A sculptural seat by Simon Verity.*

21

There is no end to innovative designs for seats: seats

swinging from trees, hewn out of stumps, mounded up out
of thyme or built into walls. There are follies where a stone
maiden offers you her lap. In seventeenth-century Holland
canny hydraulicians created startling water jets alongside a
bench. At the Villa Caprile in Italy, there was until recently
an eighteenth-century wooden seat where a concealed arm
clasped you firmly, while from his vantage point a metre
away, the jokey owner would spray you from jets. These
seats can still be bought in Italy.

22

For years I have longed to make a 'living' seat. Willow
would be best – the common crack willow *(Salix fragilis)*
which strikes so easily. Pieces pushed into the ground at
strategic places would take root in a flash and be pliable
enough to be plaited. The back and seat could be woven
into a kind of lattice work. Leafless in winter, how pretty in
spring to see one's garden seat coming alive with slender
leaves and catkins. But even more daring would be to try to
make a living seat from wisteria, where a high back would
curve over, absolutely sagging with flowers and scent. That

23

10. *The unembellished curves of the seat and table work well with the colour and design of the terrace.*

vision is wildly heady – pruning would be a nightmare. More enterprise, gusto, daring and imagination should go into the planning, designing and siting of seats from the moment that the first border is planted.

I hope the following pages will give some indication of the variety of beautiful benches there are, and that the photographs will stimulate you either to emulate what you see here, or to make original designs of your own. For convenience the photographs are grouped in the following way. All one-seater chairs are shown consecutively, including sets of dining chairs; benches for two, suitable for enclosed parts of the garden, are arranged together; followed by those for three people or more. This means that when you are looking for a seat for a specific part of the garden, you can easily see the range of that particular family. The last category is imaginative benches. They are intended to awaken ideas, to give a thrust to imagination and at the same time to prove that sitting in your garden can be as diverse as the flowers you plant.

SINGLE
SEATS

11. *What a flawless colour to put with chives.*

12. *Stylish contemporary chairs echo the bird theme from the pond.*

13. *Three chairs forming one unit.*

28

*14. Chairs for their merit rather than for
intimacy or comfort.*

15. *A Dutch-style slave seat, used for coach
drivers awaiting their masters' return.*

16. *Ryl Nowell's 'Cabbages and Kings' display at
the 1990 Chelsea Flower Show.*

17. *The colour of this rustic wood chair*
complements the grey flagstones.

18/19. *Two very successful designs for dining* al fresco.

20. *Boulevard chairs and table in a town garden. One of the best basic designs for portable garden furniture. The dark green makes it particularly attractive.*

DOUBLE SEATS

21. *A bench that has aged beautifully. Note the*
unusual tiered armrests.

22. *A quiet corner for contemplation.*

23. *The curved design of this cast-iron bench echoes the contours of the topiary* Prunus lusitanica, *and the slate-blue paintwork tones with greens and copper beech* (Fagus sylvatica purpurea) *behind.*

24. A municipal-type bench of ironwork and wood.

25. (above) *Few of us have the opportunity to make a bizarre bench out of stocks.*
26. (right) *A charming improvisation from a stone slab.*

27. *This simple bench is perhaps one of the best designs, not for comfort,*
but for grace and ageing.

28. Wood on wood. A beautiful design by Bruce Kelly for a woodland site.

SEATS FOR ALL

41

29. *A magnificent stone seat in front of a yew hedge, clipped to follow its contours.*

30. *How charming this unpainted Lutyens' seat looks, separating the blossomy background behind from formality in front.*

31. *A sinuous wooden seat set against*
a rather dull background.

32. *A stylish bench made of wood and metal.*

33. (above) *This one is unbelievable! So elegant, so upright and made for three-sided confabs.*

34. (left) *An unusual and attractive modern design.*

46

35. *A bench in long grass with water behind is
original and lovely.*

36. *This minimal seat against symmetry and*
splendour gives a brilliant effect.

48

37. *Slate is used here most effectively against*
catmint and roses.

38. *A clever idea for a small site: adobe and wood.*

39. *The different greys of this iron seat and the
cardoons work very well together.*

40. *The dark, almost black green of the bench harmonizes with the hornbeam* (Carpinus betulus) *hedge behind, and the columnar golden elms* (Ulmus 'Dampieri Ausea').

SPECIAL SITUATIONS

41. *A basic, yet effective, circular seat.*

42. *The wheels on this bench ensure easy manoeuvrability.*

54

43. *A portable seat combining its own shelter*
seems a masterly idea.

44. *Made entirely from slabs of stone, perhaps for
effect rather than comfort.*

45. *This wooden bridge has a bench built into it.*

57

46. *A Colonial-style picket fence, complete with seat.*

47. *Seats around trees have great charm. This one, undulating as it sinks into the ground, is unusual in having arms all the way round.*

48. *A wrought-iron circular seat, resplendent in*
the spring sunshine.

49. *It is quite rare to find a suitable tree from which to hang a swinging seat, and what pleasure it gives.*

50. *A resourceful seat made of stones and ivy.*

SOURCES

Some UK Addresses

Barnsley House GDF
Barnsley House
Cirencester
Gloucestershire, GL7 5EE
Telephone: (0285) 74561

Bramley Garden Furniture
4 Crittal Drive
Springwood Industrial Estate
Rayne Road
Braintree
Essex
Telephone: (0376) 20210

Lucy Fielden Furniture
66 Millman Street
London
WC1N 3EG
Telephone: (071) 405 1879

Makepeace Furniture Workshops
Parnham House
Beaminster
Dorset
Telephone: (0308) 862204

Some US Addresses

Charleston Battery Bench Inc.
191 King Street
Charleston, SC 29401
Telephone: (803) 722-3842

Country Casual
17317 Germantown Rd
Germantown, MD 20874-2999
Telephone: (301) 540-0040

Florentine Craftsmen
46-24 28th Street
Long Island City, NY 11101
Telephone: (718) 937-7632

Nampara Gardens
2004 Golf Course Road
Bayside, CA 95524
Telephone: (707) 822-5744

Smith and Hawken
25 Corte Madera
Mill Valley, CA 94941
Telephone: (415) 383-4415

Wood Classics Inc.
RD 1 Box 455E
High Falls, NY 12440
Telephone: (914) 687-7288

PICTURE CREDITS

The Publisher thanks the following photographers and
organizations for their kind permission to reproduce photographs
in this book.
Owners and designers of gardens are credited where known.
Photographers appear in bold type.

Title page. **Derek Fell**; private garden, USA

page 6. **Andrew Lawson**; Royal Horticultural Society's Gardens, Wisley, Surrey

Picture No 1 **Derek Fell**; Ohme Gardens, Wenatchee, WA, USA

Picture No 2 **Eric Crichton**; Lord Saye and Sele, Broughton Castle, Oxfordshire

Picture No 3 **Eric Crichton**; C. Crichton, Langthorns, Dorset

Picture No 4 **Eric Crichton**; Mrs M. A. Willis, Ivy Lodge

Picture No 5 **Eric Crichton**; The National Trust, Mount Stewart, County Down,
N. Ireland

Picture No 6 **Derek Fell**; private garden, USA

Picture No 7 **Hugh Palmer**; Wootton Place, Woodstock, Oxfordshire

Picture No 8 **Derek Fell**; Plantation Garden, Avery Island, Louisianna, USA

Picture No 9 **Andrew Lawson**; Designed by Simon Verity, Kiftsgate Court,
Gloucestershire

Picture No 10 **Andrew Lawson**; Chisenbury Priory, Wiltshire

Picture No 11 **George Lévêque**; Patricia-Marie van Roosmalen, Belgium

Picture No 12 **Derek Fell**; private garden, USA

Picture No 13 **Andrew Lawson**; private garden, Trebetherick, Cornwall

Picture No 14 **Eric Crichton**; The National Trust, Ham House, Surrey

Picture No 15 **Derek Fell**; private garden, Cape Town, S. Africa

Picture No 16 **Andrew Lawson**; designed by Ryl Nowell, RHS Chelsea Flower Show,
London

Picture No 17 **Derek Fell**; private garden, USA

Picture No 18 **Georges Lévêque**; Mr Guy Martin, France

Picture No 19 **Georges Lévêque**; private garden, near Fontainebleau, France

Picture No 20 **Andrew Lawson**; private garden, London

63

Picture No 21 **Derek Fell**; private garden, Great Britain

Picture No 22 **Georges Lévêque**; Denmans Garden, Fontwell, West Sussex

Picture No 23 **Eric Crichton**; The National Trust, Hidcote, Gloucestershire

Picture No 24 **Jerry Harpur**; private garden, Conndorville, Tasmania

Picture No 25 **Georges Lévêque**; Mr P. Herbert, Gravetye Manor, East Sussex

Picture No 26 **Georges Lévêque**; private garden, Belgium

Picture No 27 **Derek Fell**; Bois de Moutier, France

Picture No 28 **Jerry Harpur**; Designed by Bruce Kelly, New York, USA

Picture No 29 **Andrew Lawson**; Jenkyn Place, Bentley, Hampshire

Picture No 30 **Georges Lévêque**; Penns in the Rocks, near Groombridge, Surrey

Picture No 31 **Derek Fell**; Dumbarton Oaks, Washington DC, USA

Picture No 32 **Derek Fell**; Dumbarton Oaks, Washington DC, USA

Picture No 33 **Andrew Lawson**; Dalemain, Penrith, Cumbria

Picture No 34 **Andrew Lawson**; Kellie Castle, Fife, Scotland

Picture No 35 **Georges Lévêque**; Abbots Ripton Hall, Huntington, Yorkshire

Picture No 36 **Hugh Palmer**; Vaux-le-Vicomte, France

Picture No 37 **Hugh Palmer**; Arley Hall, Near Northwich, Cheshire

Picture No 38 **Derek Fell**; Carmel Mission Garden, Carmel, CA, USA

Picture No 39 **Derek Fell**; Huntington Botanical Garden, CA, USA

Picture No 40 **Georges Lévêque**; Patricia-Marie van Roosmalen, Belgium

Picture No 41 **Andrew Lawson**; private garden, London

Picture No 42 **Andrew Lawson**; The National Trust, Powis Castle, Welshpool, Wales

Picture No 43 **Eric Crichton**; Mrs S. Spencer, York Gate, Leeds, Yorkshire

Picture No 44 **Andrew Lawson**; Levens Hall, Kendal, Cumbria

Picture No 45 **Derek Fell**; Governor's Palace, Colonial Williamsburg,
Washington DC, USA

Picture No 46 **Derek Fell**; Governor's Palace, Colonial Williamsburg,
Washington DC, USA

Picture No 47 **Eric Crichton**; Countess of Salisbury, Hatfield House, Hertfordshire

Picture No 48 **Derek Fell**; Ladew Garden, Baltimore, MD, USA

Picture No 49 **Derek Fell**; private garden, California, USA

Picture No 50 **Derek Fell**; private garden, USA